SLOW IS FAST

Dan Malloy
Kanoa Zimmerman
& Kellen Keene

patagonia®

Ventura, California

ON THE ROAD AT HOME

My moment of awakening was on the PCH approaching Big Sur. I was high as a kite on shitty coffee, burping up an oversized burrito, and pedaling hard toward a looming incline when, through a haze of endorphins, I heard myself blurt out, "I've been carsick for thirty-four years!"

It wouldn't be the last time that Kanoa and Kellen would accommodatingly smirk at one of my kooky exclamations while huffing and puffing up a steep grade.

Twelve years ago, preparing to board a fifteen-hour flight to Indonesia, I stood before a giant wall of magazines searching for something to read. The usual tempting bullshit dominated my field of view. Stuffed in the back, in a negative space that drew me toward it, was a slim black-and-white periodical without a single advertisement called *The Sun*. Inside there was an interview with author and farmer Wendell Berry.

He explained that industrialized agriculture has inflicted "a kind of cultural amnesia" on our society. The chasm between the people growing our food and the people eating it (us) is a modern phenomenon that is doing more damage to our communities and to the surrounding environment than we are capable of quantifying.

Mr. Berry's work has changed how I see my place in this world. It has taught me that deliberate participation in healthy food and fiber systems is a different kind of social and environmental activism that requires more working for and less fighting against—same goals, just less bureaucracy and fewer bumper stickers.

He suggests that universities should be teaching our youth how to return home—to take care of their families, their communities, their farmland, and the wild places that surround them—rather than encouraging them to flee their birthplaces in pursuit of corporate fraternities. This made perfect sense but shattered the foundation of my current occupation; I was in the midst of a fifteen-year career traveling the world as a professional surfer. I was already uneasy about the mechanisms that were enabling this pursuit of glorified recreation, and somehow his words solidified this need for a homecoming of sorts that had been slowly welling up in me.

I couldn't quit traveling cold turkey so I called Kanoa and Kellen to see if they were up for hitting the road at home, a self-prescribed attempt to cure our own cultural amnesia. The prescription: no progress toward our destination by car, no hotels, no computers, and no social media.

We were desperately nostalgic for the road trips of twenty years ago, when a good photograph was not the destination but evidence of a good adventure. A time when darkness meant the cameras were put away. When preparing dinner meant people working together and telling tall tales to the pulse of flame-licked shadows. Back when the closest thing to GPS was a decent map or a local's imperfect drawing in the dirt.

In a way, I really had been carsick for thirty-four years. Not nauseous, but disconnected.

Soon after we departed, I realized that travel by bicycle isn't just slower and more deliberate, it also forces you to constantly reckon with all of your senses. My vigilance was sharpened by each pothole, each passing semi, each sage-filled breeze. We could feel the weather warming as we made our way south, and the severity of our soreness was directly correlated to each mile of progress.

Something about the self-contained transient mode seemed to cultivate serendipity—locals received us with an openness that I had never experienced before in California. Maybe it was because we were passing through, not blowing by. – *Dan Malloy, April 2017*

FOREWORD

Heading north on the Coast Starlight from Ventura to Oakland, four Amish girls two seats ahead quietly practice beautiful gospel songs. Behind me two old men are getting drunk on wine and also singing, but I can't tell what.

There wasn't enough rain this winter so the hills are turning gold early. Rolling into the San Joaquin Valley we pass giant monoculture farms with perfectly straight GPS rows that disappear into the horizon. Not a weed in sight. Running next to the 101 we pass King City, Greenfield, Soledad, and Salinas. The train yards bloom with graffiti. I keep my eyes peeled for ghost markings by Matokie Slaughter or Bozo Texino.

Again I hear the drunkards rambling and the soft whisper of the Amish quartet.

The old-timers start arguing. Now there is a guy from Texas, one from Arizona, and another from San Francisco. They argue loudly about intelligent design, terrorism, the general good, and a lack of good neighbors. "We can live without oil, we can't live without water!"

The Amish girls aren't singing any more. I can't help but to guess that they think we are completely crazy. Every modern crisis the old-timers are bellowing about, the Amish seem to have steered clear of.

Midmorning tomorrow we will get dropped off 100 miles north of San Francisco with our bikes, a bag of film, one surfboard, a few cameras, flippers, a two-man tent, and wetsuits. The pages that follow are a document of our 700-mile journey back home.

– Dan Malloy

ROAD OF DREAMS
By Steve Barilotti

A horseman high—alone as an eagle on the spur of the
mountain over Mirmas Canyon draws rein, looks down at
the bridge builders, the power shovels, the teeming end of
the new coast road at the mountain's base. He sees the loops
of the road go northward, headland beyond headland, into
great mist over Fraser's Point, he shakes his fist and makes the
gesture of wringing a chicken's neck, scowls and rides higher.
– Robinson Jeffers, "The Coast-Road," 1938

The road owns a certain archaeology. Dig through the
aggregate deep enough and you will likely uncover the
strata of historical transit and the vanished people it
carried. California's prehistoric coastal road would have
been a spidery, intermittent web of tribal footpaths
beginning in Baja California and traveling north through
coastal bands such as the Kumeyaay, Chumash, Salinan,
Esselen, and Miwok. Conquistadores and cattle chose the
path of least resistance. Mission oxcarts followed, then
Yankee farm wagons that further rutted the coastal road.
Like a coral reef building on the skeletons of the past,
accreting asphalt and concrete, aligning, straightening out
the kinks, mathematically defining optimal radius and
bank over time.

Life, or at least the curious bits worth noting, seems
to proliferate best along borders of flux and disruption.
Ecologists call it the Edge Effect. Evolution occurs harder,
faster, and more ruthlessly on the interface of seeming crisis
... one adapts to fast-changing conditions and thrives, or
quickly becomes part of the fossil record. On the North
American west coast, the edge is very much alive. It

wriggles, shimmies, and squirms … upthrusts and subducts
and falls off into the ocean in huge wanton chunks.
Relentless waves generated by Aleutian storms invariably
align with peak tides to lash sodden cliff faces, the cobble-
spiked whitewash chewing away acres of soft sedimentary
rock and triggering wholesale collapse. The edge chews
houses, eats roads. It doesn't play nice with notions like
private property and Manifest Destiny. And it likely is the
worst-case scenario for building a major scenic byway.

But without the Pacific Coast Highway, California
would be a landlocked Midwest colony, with no more
sexy coastal culture than Canada. PCH was built for
romance and land speculation, a whimsical tourist's
road linking together isolated fishing villages and sleepy
vacation enclaves like trinkets on a charm bracelet. Over
the decades it morphed into an analog information
highway that carried surfers, iconic California lifestyle,
and a burgeoning modern counterculture along America's
western edge.

Originally cobbled together in 1919 from a disparate
collection of fragmented coastal roads, PCH took eighteen
years to build, applying ingenuity, convict muscle, and
sheer arrogance to carve a road shelf into the belly of
steep, storm-pounded palisades. Along the 100-mile
Big Sur stretch, supplies and steam shovels were ferried
from narrow doghole anchorages and winched up to the
construction site using steam-powered donkey engines.
Landslides were frequent, raining boulders on men and
equipment, sending tractors tumbling into the surf 200
feet below.

But by the time highway workers connected the last section in 1937 they had saddle-broken the wild California coast for speedy automobile transit. Completed in the depths of the Great Depression as the jewel of WPA engineering, it became a Road of Dreams for a broken, dispirited nation.

Surfers were early adopters, drafting quickly in PCH's slipstream to access previously closed sections of coast like Malibu and Secos. By the late 1930s the weekend club surfari enabled young Depression-era surfers to sample new breaks and mingle with isolated surf tribes from San Diego to San Francisco. In the process, surfers created an alternative oral geography of seaside California … renaming beaches and coastal topography according to whim and unfiltered observation. "Crumple Car," "Chasms," "Oil Piers," "Beacons," "Birdshit."

Along PCH, called Cabrillo Highway north of Santa Cruz to San Francisco, small family farms conclude abruptly off irregular fingers of crumbling palisades. Pacific Rim agriculture, sea farmers who survey a turbulent ocean horizon from the wheelhouse of their tractor seat; watch distant ships pass, pelicans draft twenty deep along the cliff's edge. A frost-free coastal terrace, perfect for fog-loving, salt-tolerant brassicas … pungent broccoli and cauliflower, cabbages, asparagus, artichokes. Cosmic logarithmic spirals of Romanesco … yellow dusting of mustard flowers between the rows.

This afternoon a trio of bike campers—Dan Malloy, Kanoa Zimmerman, and Kellen Keene—are cruising the flat stretch fronting Four Mile on the last approach into Santa Cruz. They are four days out of San Francisco, 200 miles total since they started in Point Arena three weeks earlier. Dan's bike is trailing a canary-yellow squashtail together with his cameras and camping kit. Kanoa and Kellen are hauling film and video gear.

The project, dubbed "Slow Is Fast," mingles biking, photography, surfing, and visiting family farms and assorted old-school artisans along PCH. They have always wanted to explore and document the overlooked corners of their home state's coastline … the blurry bits usually whooshed by in the rush to find photogenic star waves.

The surf they've found so far has been unremarkable, yet after a long afternoon's grind, just rinsing off in the chilly shorebreak takes on a baptismal quality. Every wave, no matter how flawed or gutless, becomes a gift. Small flakes of color sifted from unlikely pockets, recalibrating sights for fun, not glory. A small voyage of rediscovery, moving slowly … exposed enough to imagine that highway worker eighty years ago … him, first up, coffee by oil lamp, feeling the fog, hearing pines rustle, clatter of unseen cobbles far below in the splash zone.

The bikes allow ready stealth access to pristine camping setups, starlit pirate coves straight out of a Stevenson adventure. Wrack and tangle and the perfume of bubbling soup, kelp, wet neoprene, grandfather sage, mussel ovum, small driftwood fires. Summing up a surfing life, all along these salt roads, the millions of waves observed, some felt, fewer still ridden.

Collective road memory. Back to that first and best place when the greatest adventure lay just one break up the beach.

LEGEND

MOUNTAINS	
OUR ROUTE	
RIVER	
COUNTY LINE	
CAMP	
FARM	
HOUSE	
NEAT MISC	
OLEAN	
TRAIN	

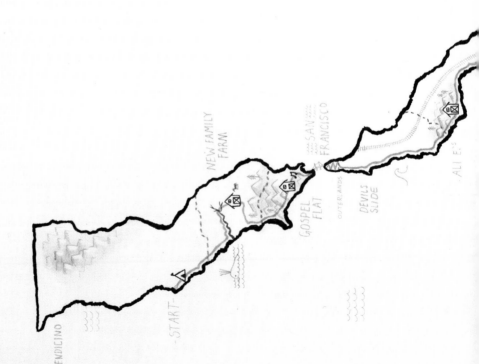

MENDICINO

-START-

GOSPEL FLAT

NEW FAMILY FARM

SAN FRANCISCO

OUTER LANDS

DEVILS SLIDE

ALI E.

SC

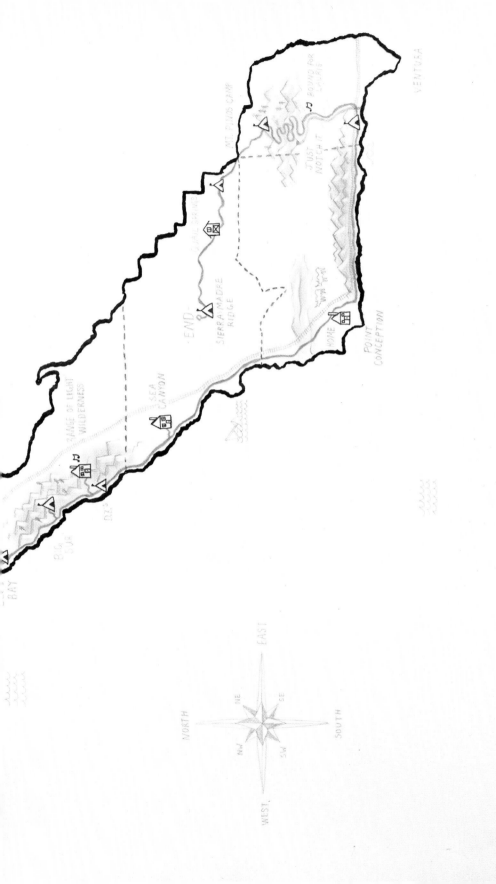

(Above)
Day 1: Danny Hess, San Francisco–based surfer, shaper, artist, and
reliable resource, transported crew and gear from Oakland train
station to 100 miles north of San Francisco in Mendocino County.

(Right)
First session.

ADAM DAVIDOFF AND RYAN POWER
New Family Farm, Sebastopol

Over the last twenty years, real horsepower has rebounded steadily as an increasing number of new and veteran farmers rediscover the inherent benefits of using draft animals.

Dan: Why did you get into using horses?

Adam: It felt like they had a lot to teach us. Like patience, and patience, and patience and humility. And some more patience, and all that sort of thing.

Ryan: The more nonhuman partnerships I foster, the more human I feel.

MICKEY MURCH AND BRONWEN HALSEY MURCH

Gospel Flat Farm, Bolinas

Dan: **How did you end up farming here?**

Mickey: I became a farmer after realizing that art is much bigger than what you hang on a wall in a gallery. I realized that there was a network—or a whole subset—of art that was outside of the gallery, and that is where I came from.

Dan: **What does the concept of sustainability mean to you?**

Mickey: I think sustainability means not burning out; finding something you can improve upon and making it more efficient. I also see it as incorporating more of your family into your everyday work schedule.

Dan: **Tell me about the evolution of the farmstand.**

Mickey: When I first started farming here, it was the artist versus the producer. My dad was the producer and I was the artist. We gradually created the farmstand. It started with this little tent where we put extra cabbages, and then it kept growing. The farmstand was this healer between my father and me because suddenly the farmstand started moving so much produce that there was no need to wholesale it. He was happy because we could move the produce, and I was happy because the farmstand is a total cultural artwork.

The farmstand is this solidifier for all of the family energy. It's brought my grandparents back in because there's always something for them to do, like trimming weeds and making bouquets. And it's been the link that's really solved this problem

of "how do we share everything?" in the relationship between my dad and me. If we hadn't decided to trust people and have that be where we were in our hearts—trusting everyone who drives by, putting the best of our produce out there on the honor system—then the farmstand couldn't exist.

Dan: **The other day you were talking about growing food as activism, as compared with other forms, such as protest or political activism. Can you talk about that?**

Mickey: When you're a farmer and you talk about farming, you feel like you can touch base with any American. No matter how blue or red they are, everyone has a farm somewhere back in their ancestry, or their uncle has a farm, or they've tried to grow

a tomato and can commiserate about how hard it is to grow something. Suddenly you're connected to everybody, and it's not about who's wealthy and who's not; it's that growing food is this ultimate glue, and it can connect people.

I think life is more about creating these connections than bemoaning which percentile we're in or how we've been struck down by various forces at work. There's this joy to feeling a connection to people, and I think that's more of what I work with, rather than fleshing out the disconnect, which is what a lot of protest is about.

(Left)
A respite between the fields and the farmstand.
(Above)
Potato harvest.

(Above)
Vegetable bodyguard, 2:00 a.m.

Day 15: Mill Valley

(Above)

Brett Simundson and Alexi Glickman of Magic West.

(Above, right, and previous spread)
Day 17: San Francisco

DANNY HESS
San Francisco

***Dan:* Why wood?**

Danny Hess: I was never out to make a really beautiful surfboard. I was looking to reengineer the surfboard in a better way and find better materials. I wanted to make a surfboard that felt more natural to a surfer and lasted ten times longer. When I was growing up riding conventional foam surfboards, it broke my heart when a magic board would wear out after six months.

I'd like to continue that path toward a more indestructible, heirloom-type board. It could be something that's like a guitar.

Something that has a certain resonance and a certain sound to it that you become very attached to.

The redwood board that Dan was riding yesterday was an attempt at taking old salvaged redwood and manipulating it into a functional surfboard. That thing is just hollowed, glued redwood that's shaped and finished with linseed oil. It totally works, it's a functional surfboard, it's heavy as hell.

(Previous spread)
Traditional sign maker, Jeff Canham, and custom furniture builder, Luke Bartels and Banjo. Woodshop, San Francisco.

(Following spread)
Barry McGee retrospective, Berkeley Art Museum.

Monday	Tuesday	Wednesday	Thursday	Friday	Saturday	Sunday
week 35					S&D NATIVE @ GOSPEL FLAT.	12
					1	2
week 36	GOSPEL FLATS TO BIG Fog SAN MT. TAM	MILL VALLEY TRUE LABS RECORDING	MILL VALLEY REST	S.F.	SF	19.
13		4	5	6	8	9
3						
week 37		DPRT S.F. TO H.M.B.	S.F. TO SAN MATEO	BANDE MATEO SURF HMOUGE RENTAL THEN TO ATHES	SANTA CRUZ WESTSIDE MARKET DINNER W/ALL	S.C. HMB LARRY INTERVIEW BODY SURF
20 21						
10	11	12	13	14	15	16
S.C. TO TOST HOLLOW JUNILE WAVE TRACK W/ TIFF	TRACK W/ TIFF 28	S.C. TO M. VALLEY VAN TO ANDREW	ANDREW M.U W/ JACK ESPER TREVOR	ANDREW M. TO DARTH RIDGE	DART. RIDGE TO ESALON TO BASKET	BASKET SOME 32
17	18				22	23
week 39	D&2? LIGHT HOUSE TO S.C. LIGHT HOUSE	LIGHT HOUSE TO S.C.	SEE CANYON JALAMA 37	38	JALAMA 39	JALAND 40
24	25	26	27	28	29	30

notes

WALK OR
BOARD SHORT WETSUIT

Monday	Tuesday	Wednesday	Thursday	Friday	Saturday	Sunday
	SEE CANYON	SURF JALAMA	JALAMA TO SAN JULIAN	SAN JULIAN TO FARIA	FARIA TO OJAI	LAURIE FUND RAISER @ LIBBEY BOWL
1	2	3	4	5	6	
	UP THE 33 TO PINE MTN	MEET GRAHAM S.B. CANYON TO DICK OG.	S.B. CANYON TO CHIMINEAZ	CHIMINEA TO QUAIL SPRINGS	Q.S.	Q.S. TO OJAI
	MART		11	12	13	14
55 56 57		END		HANOX HOOUM EL CAP		
15	16	17	18	19	20	21
22	23	24	25	26	27	28
week 44	30	31				

notes

4 SHAKAS   STILL WATER PAN HANDLE MONTERA

O MIDDLE FINGERS

2 ANGRY HONKS

MULTIPLE INTHUSED HONKS

(Right)

Contemporary flintknapped dacite knife by Jack Harrison.
Currently used for skinning large game. Harrison, twenty-four,
has been traditionally crafting prehistoric tools for over ten years
and has been commissioned by the UC Berkeley Archaeology
department to replicate coastal California native artifacts.

(Left)

Tiffany Morgan Campbell, Bonny Doon, Santa Cruz. Campbell s a filmmaker, skateboarder, surfer, writer, teacher, and co-author f *Animal Tracking Basics.*

(Above, clockwise)

lack Bear *(Ursus americanus)*, Raccoon *(Procyon lotor)*, urfer *(Northern californicas dudicus).*

Cruz.

Freedman (cofounder, Dirty
ll, Ali Edwards (cofounder,

(Above)
Big Ag.
(Right)
Small Ag.

Jeff Larkey, farmer (following spread, seventh from right): "I don't think we're going to be able to depend on our leaders or our political people to warn us in advance because I think their ~~rests~~ lie elsewhere. So it's good to start thinking about it before ~~s~~ really difficult to maintain any kind of independence. ~~verything~~ will be dictated to us because the ~~'~~ there. I started growing food because I felt ~~ndent~~ thing I could do."

~~d,~~ third from right):
~~~kes time to really
~~ause community is

Dave Gardner, farmer (following spread, second from right): "This stuff takes a whole lot of hard work, but it's not rocket science. It's hard and it's mysterious and it's frustrating and it's heartbreaking at times. But having the experience early on of watching things grow and eating them or saving them is invaluable. Farming's not just some mysterious thing that shows up in a plastic box. Everybody can love the computer world and the game world and all that stuff, but I think it's about 97 percent worthless, and not reality and reactionary and a waste. But it's not like everybody has to be a farmer and not everybody has to have a garden, but it's fun. It's fun to plant stuff; it's fun to clean stuff up; it's fun to eat your own stuff in the yard. It's not going to save the world, but if people live better lives, that's better than if they don't live better lives."

Day 29: Big Sur

Surf travel is by practice nonlinear. To find a good wave, one slowly traces a variegated coastline; meandering, halting, backtracking. Steinbeck called it *vacilando*—setting out for somewhere but not particularly concerned about getting there. It was on PCH that California surfers seeking a vanished frontier manifested a seminomadic life, tracking swell like Plains Indians following the buffalo migration … heeding the road poetry of Whitman, Jeffers, Guthrie, and Kerouac … skirting the edge where the march of Manifest Destiny sputtered to a halt and stumbled headfirst into a deep, mystic Pacific. Facing west, looking east … the end of America … surfing's Beat Highway. – *Steve Barilotti*

(Previous spread)
Santa Cruz farm and water folk.

(Above)
Home and recording studio of The Range of Light Wilderness.

(Right)
L-R: Tommy McDonald, Nick Aives, and Jessi Campbell
on Partington Ridge, Big Sur.

(Above)
Trevor Gordon.

(Right, lower left)
Van life.

(Right, lower right)
Cold Makaha.

DAVID ZWEIFEL
Big Sur

David Zweifel, "DZ," is a Big Sur local and teacher who, as he likes to joke, works "full-time-part-time" driving the school bus and working maintenance at the Esalen Institute. He is a sculptor, construction worker, carpenter, swim coach, lifeguard, concrete worker, ceramicist, tool-wrencher, camp host, preserve manager, surfer, and ax thrower. He lives with his dog, Esperanza, among the tree folk caretaking a house on a secluded former gold mining canyon.

Dan: **What do you like about teaching?**

DZ: I like talking with the kids about learning to interpret what they see. I ask them, what are you really seeing? Or what do you think you're seeing? And what are you looking at? How does it make these colors? You might just assume that everything is green, but if you look closely at the trees, there are greens and whites and blues.

Dan: **How did you learn to surf?**

Around 1968 I went to Pismo Beach with my dad. He rented me a surfboard and said, "Go at it," so I went out. It was freezing cold, and I just got fully thrashed. I didn't have a clue, but when I came in I just thought to myself, *That was great!*

Then my mom went to Hawai'i, and I got to go for three weeks. Waikiki was within walking distance of our little hotel. I didn't know anyone so I just sat on the beach and listened to how all the beach boys talked. They were tanned as hell with red shorts on. I was clueless in the water, always getting in the way. In the lineup, one Hawaiian guy rang my bell. He said, "Come here,

kid! How old are you?" And I was like, "Um ... fourteen," and he just goes boom! I was like, oh, okay I get it now. I didn't feel like it was a mean thing really, it was just like, "Wake up, kid!" With some kids, a little knock on the head gets them on a better path. From then on I was way more focused.

Dan: **How did you get into throwing hatchets?**

DZ: Kids will make guns out of anything. If you don't give them guns then fingers and sticks and everything else becomes guns. They're shooting each other and playing these war games. And it just seemed really weird. I appreciated and respected guns when I was young. They are fun, and I know the draw to that energy. But I was trying to look for an alternative to that kind of energy for my kids; something thrilling that would appeal to them and requires a ton of skill and concentration. And so we got into throwing axes and knives. It really caught their imagination. One of the boys likes knives, one likes tomahawks, and one likes big axes because he's a great big kid. And of course we all want to throw them as far as possible and stick them.

Dan: **Any accidents?**

DZ: No accidents. Not even any particularly close calls that I can think of. You have to exert a great amount of physical effort to do it, which eliminates a lot of the random accidental possibilities. It's fun, and I realized it was sort of meditation. If I can't go surfing it calms me down, helps me focus my thinking. It's medicine.

Day 37: San Luis Obispo

(Above)
Don Andrade, bladesmith
San Luis Obispo

(Right)
Buzz Morasca, surfer, rescue sled fabricator
San Luis Obispo

"My bladesmithing has become a big part of my own spiritual practice. If the power goes out I can still make a knife with a small coal forge. It's really liberating. It's a lot slower but it's a lot more accurate and safer. The reason I'm wearing this patch on my finger today is strictly a result of a power tool. And the slower, meditative approach always yields a much higher quality product.

I feel like I make heirloom-quality knives that could be passed down from one generation to the next. Knives are almost the antithesis of fine art sculpture. It's this beautiful thing, but it becomes an integral part of your well-being."

"I build practical things from what's available. I don't like to spend a lot of money, so I design from resource. 'Design from resource' is a term used in architecture that means trying to repurpose and recycle readily available materials. My friend Randy affectionately calls it 'Buzz tech.' I call it 'chicken salad from chicken shit.'"

(Above)
Dan.

(Right)
Chad Jackson, archaeologist.

(Above)
Megan Hooker, Brittany Smith, Grace Malloy, and Mariko Reed.
One hour after birth, postpartum cuddlefest, Lompoc.

(Above)
John Fulton at Pacific Coast Lumber Mill in San Luis Obispo.

(Right)
Don Seawater, owner.

(Above)
Freediver, diesel mechanic, and commercial rock cod fisherman
Eric Hodge with his father.

(Right)
Aboard seventeen-foot Greenough-designed vessel in Gaviota.

Making ends meet as a small-scale farmer requires more creativity than ever. Other than farming the best produce in town, Steve Sprinkel self-publishes the *Forager*, a weekly one-sheet that lets his customers know what's happening on the farm and why. Ojai, Ventura County.

FORAGER

watermelon follies

22 August 2012

Watermelons can be hard to trust. Like most melons, they are secretive, closed, impervious to your curiosity. Are you ripe? The watermelon shrugs. Actually, you will be lucky if it even does that, because they don't even care. They give little hint if they are ready or not. But they look ready. Then you make a fool of yourself. Most melons are not that austere. A cantaloupe is not coy. You can tell a ripe cantaloupe from two meters away. Its color tells you its ready, and as if there was any doubt, the melon slips right off the vine the second you pick it up. If it wants to stay it will let you know. And you should listen because when you get it home you may be in for a big green disappointment.

I was cock sure I had the whole watermelon thing down until this year. I would show off and talk real big about all my broad experience in the world of ripe watermelons.

" No," I would caution," you can't tell much by thumping them unless, I suppose, you have had a lot of experience thumping fields of watermelons." I smirk smugly at pretenders, thumping watermelons at the farmers market, vainly plumbing ripeness with sonar.

In the past I have been disdainful of the southern thumpers. We are not known for our watermelon prowess in the west, but anyone from Texas to the Carolinas considers themselves one savvy watermelon thumper. They're the Dudamels of finely tuned melons. I still don't know what they are supposed to sound like, even though I have wandered around in a field of Texas watermelon in Gause (Milam County) with a recognized melon maestro named Larry Butler.

" Now see, what you're looking for is a C sharp. If you have a C flat or if it's stuck in B it'd not be worth hauling out of the field. And anything that sounds like A is just for target practice."

Larry thumped out something that I hoped was C, but he left the thirty pounder Royal Sweet on the ground to grow a few notes sweeter.

" Here ya go." He said. " Listen to this." He thumped the middle of the melon with a practiced hand. The sound it made could have been hollow bamboo, a marimba or maybe the sound a nail makes when it strikes a metal stanchion you failed to account for. Seemed like there was a good measure of faith involved in selecting and mine was blind. When Larry cut the melon open on the kitchen table, we knew there was no reason to doubt that we would have red perfection.

I don't remember how I learned about the tendril. I have used the Burnt Tendril 4.0 method of watermelon selection for the last four or five years and gained much confidence. To wit: adjoining the watermelon stem there be a curled tendril half an inch long that is meant to grasp a supporting tree branch where the melon is growing, perhaps 8 million years ago in the wild of south central Africa. The tendril is a wiry, coiled appendment, seemingly more delicate than it's role would suggest, hanging a big ball of water off the ground so it would not be consumed by wild pigs and tortoises.

When the tendril is brown, the melon is ripe. When it is ripe, the tendril breaks, the melon falls, and 8 million years ago the viable seeds explode out of the bulky bomb. Helpful beasts, some winged, carry the sweet flesh filled with seeds far and wide to propagate the fruit in another space.

But Burnt Tendril 4.0 needs an upgrade. Or at least the Sugar Baby Sandia program patch. My tendrils are deceiving me. All the green Sugar Baby watermelons don't have tendrils. Some tendrils that are newly burnt are on over ripe melons. Some that seem burnt enough to be ripe are white. We blame all the confusion on the recent two weeks of hot weather. We have performed field surgery on quite a few in order to learn more and salvage best what we can. Forget the thumping. I tried that too. We remain unsure. That is why the boxes of watermelons are piled up outside, as if they are not fit for the CSA delivery room. Take one home and be part of the mystery. Today I heard a few melons speak to me, telling me of their perfect ripeness, and when sure I cut one down the center. I was not disappointed and I hope you too will not be. We will have more melons on offer next week, so if you got a bad one you can have another. We are The Farmer and The Cook, home of the Melon Back Guarantee.

(Above)
Rincon surf and camp, Ventura County.

(Previous spread)
Emma Wood. Not visible: Tim Curran.

MATILIJA DAM
Ojai

Ojai Valley's Matilija dam, constructed in 1948 for farming and water storage, quickly silted up, choking off natural river flow and critical sediment transport. By 1964 it was condemned, but nearly fifty years later the dam remains, due to political shortsightedness and bureaucratic foot-dragging. Locals have been working since the 1970s to implement an orderly takedown of the dam to restore native steelhead migration routes and put critically needed sand back on Ventura's beaches. Although politically incorrect and illegal, the dam was a great place to cool off on the last grind up to Cuyama Valley.

(Above)

On day 52, Kellen contracted severe food poisoning at a
biker eatery en route to Cuyama. Three days later he was sick,
dehydrated, and unable to ride the last ten miles. Thanks to
pistachio farmer John Karam, the team arrived safely at the
gates of Quail Springs Permaculture farm.

BRENTON KELLY AND JAN SMITH

Quail Springs Permaculture Site and Educational Center, Maricopa

Dan: **How did you become involved with Quail Springs?**

Jan Smith: I read *The One-Straw Revolution* by Masanobu Fukuoka, a Japanese farmer, about ten or eleven years ago, and it planted a seed. I just felt like the direction of my life needed simplicity and extremely basic relationships. All of a sudden I had this thing come up in me. For many women it is, "I've got to have a baby." But for me it was, "I've got to know how to grow food."

Brenton Kelly: Personally, I didn't want to be participating directly in the paradigm that is the standard world out there. So I was thinking I could just live up in a cave in the mountains, but then I thought I'd miss getting up on the soapbox and sharing the work I'm doing. So living and teaching out here in a remote wilderness setting with social interchange has been a beautiful thing.

Dan: **What do you love most about what you do?**

Jan: I just really love soil, and I really love light. I feel like I've done a lot of things in my life to find God or truth or real basic connections with life. Growing food seems to be the most simple and direct way I've found to explore my spirituality; to explore who I am and what I'm becoming. I think I'm a strange breed; I think I'm pretty much a wild critter.

Brenton: The beautiful thing about permaculture is that it addresses energy, food, shelter, and water—all things that sustain us.

Dan: **What's been a major turning point for you?**

Jan: After getting arrested for protesting the Iraq war, I realized that for me the highest form of activism I could do was to feed people. It's hard to explain, but for me the best work I can think of is just saying, "Hey, are you hungry? Do you need some food? Do you want to sit down and have some water?" I feel like that makes people become themselves.

Brenton: One of the things I really love to share is demystifying the aspects of food production and natural building homesteads. It can be executed very simply. People come out here with the notion that we are living in mud houses and dirt farming. But we have a satellite link, we have Internet, we have laser-perforated drip tape. We also have lightweight nylon electric fencing for predator control that I can move myself so we can keep livestock out on pasture.

Dan: **Anything else?**

Brenton: I'd love to keep chatting, but I have to take the goats for a walk.

Day 57: Cuyama

Dick Gibford (pictured left) lives alone in a cow camp high in the Sierra Madre. Life for him is his cattle and horses, but there is no die-cut sticker on his old truck that reads "Cowboy Up!" The reason being, Dick's not a cowboy.

Everything the American cowboy is today comes directly from the Spanish vaquero, who bred horses and cattle in California at least a hundred years before the Texas cowpuncher archetype ever existed. There was no Spanish equivalent of "git 'er done" for the vaqueros. Their mantra was the opposite: "poco a poco," or little by little. They took the time they needed to do things in their traditional way and took pride in moving their cattle slowly as not to stress them. The vaqueros worked countless hours braiding masterful rawhide bridles and ropes and spent their lives working with horses as their partners, not their servants. They were known to treat their horses better than themselves and they found the process in which they worked just as important as what they accomplished.

If cowboys are a dying breed, vaqueros are on the verge of extinction. When Dick was young, he rode with some of the last of the vaqueros.

He learned to braid rawhide with them and how to patiently bring a young horse straight up into the bridle. He saw the boom and bust of the cattle business and chose to have less, take his time, and carry on the tradition of the vaquero.

In the spring he'll occasionally come out of the hills to help on neighboring ranches. Oftentimes the young cowboys with their nylon ropes will be whooping and hollering right out of the gates. They'll be running their horses flat out after cattle as they dive through creeks and into the brush, scattering them into the distance.

And oftentimes 'ol Dick will head out by himself, his horse at a walk. At the end of the day, more times than not, he'll show up at the corral with more cattle than all the young bucks put together. His horse still at a walk, and the cattle not spooked or stressed. He'll follow the last calf through the gate, rub his horse's neck in appreciation and grin, "poco a poco amigo, slow is fast."
– *Chris Malloy*

And as he climbed back up the hill
The night was clear and still
And time was something far away
So he stopped to watch and listen
Under stars so bright they glistened
And he studied them and the way those patterns lay.

Then he saw one fall and burn
Never to return
And he wondered,
Was another star being born?
Then a man-made satellite
Floated slowly across the path that shootin' star had torn.

So he thought about that awhile
And damn! He had to smile
About how man was closing in all around
Then he saw his campfire flicker
And he heard a horse nicker
And the tinkling of the bell
Was the only other sound.

He was just glad to be
Way out here
Still somewhat free
From pressure to conform
To modern times.
And if they wanted to find him out
They had better map a better route
And scrutinize the print between the lines.

Excerpted from *While An Eagle Soared Like A Desert Lord*
By Dick Gibford

Dan Malloy: Mexican-Irish from Ojai, California.
Kellen Keene: Irish-Italian filmmaker and commercial fisherman, currently living in San Luis Obispo, California.
Kanoa Zimmerman: Jewish-Hawaiian, currently living and working in San Francisco, California.

Acknowledgments: Grace Malloy, Mariko Reed, Kelly Metcalf, Monika McClure, Jeff McElroy, Alyssa Firmin, Ali Edwards, Trevor Gordon, Foster Huntington, Vincent Stanley, the Chouinard family, the Metcalf family, Tiffany and Thomas Campbell, Dmitri Siegel, Jeff Johnson, Jason Frazier, Matt Stoecker, Emma Wood, Graham Goodfield, Jim and Robin Brady, Devon Bella, Todd Hannigan, Xocoyotzin Moraza, Fernando Apodaca, Jason Mariani, Jonathan McEuen, Ben Lemke, the Pata family, the Bueti family, the Malloy family, the Brittingham family, the Turner family, the Keene family, the Zimmerman family, Chris Del Moro, Coley Glasgow, Evan Daniels, Ian McGee, Tim Lynch, Mike Pizzo, Fuji, Jane Seivert, Jenning Steger, the McAnany family, Jon Swift, Steiny, the Tappis family, Kasey Kersnoski, Marco, The Mob Shop, the Mattson family, Michael Harbert, Dave Sanchez, Lisa Iida, the Montgomery family, the Lennon family, Jason McCaffrey, Luke and Joanne Bartels, Slaid Cleaves, Jack Halloway, FCD, Adam T, Macy Price, the Murch family, the Halsey family, Belle Bueti, Kyle Field, Lisa Brey, the Burkard family, Steve Sprinkel, Devon Howard, Karla Olson. And a special thanks to all the people we met along the way.

Dedicated to the memory of Bob Isaacson.

Principal photography: Kanoa Zimmerman
Contributing photographers: Chris Burkard, Kellen Keene, Dan Malloy, Mariko Reed
Book Design: Jeff Canham
Editor: Steve Barilotti
Proofreading: Mia Sullivan, Britton Caillouette, Grace Malloy
Map (page 8): Trevor Gordon

patagonia

Published by Patagonia Books®
Patagonia publishes a select number of titles on wilderness, wildlife, and outdoor sports that inspire and restore a connection to the natural world.

Slow Is Fast / Malloy / Zimmerman / Keene
ISBN 978-1-938340-74-1
Library of Congress Control Number: 2014930890

One percent of sales from this book go to the preservation and restoration of the natural environment.